The Ultimate Law Student Get-A-Job Checklist

A step-by-step guide to help *every* student land a great job

By
Ross Fishman, JD
Fishman Marketing, Inc.

Edited by
Kerriann Stout, Esq.
Vinco Bar Exam Coaching

Testimonials

*"This book offers **incredibly clear and useful advice** for students or new grads who want to maximize their career search!"*

Hollis R Hanover, J.D.
Associate Director of Career Services
Loyola University Chicago School of Law

*"An easy to read, **insightful, and honest** look at how to tackle law school."*

Brittany Kaplan
J.D. Candidate 2019
Chicago-Kent College of Law

*"This book provides **extraordinarily powerful insight** to law students, regardless of their class rank."*

Samantha Ruben
J.D. Candidate 2019
IIT Chicago-Kent College of Law

*"**This book totally saved me.** I got a much better job than I ever thought I could."*

Michael, J.D., Class of 2018

*"I not only got a great job, I got it working in Banking Law, which is **my passion!**"*

Matthew, J.D., Class of 2018

*"This book is **pure genius**. Until I read the Get-A-Job Checklist, it had never occurred to me to approach getting hired this way. **It works!**"*

Jessica, J.D., Class of 2017

*"I'm in the bottom-half of a mid-tier law school. But **I got a great 2L summer job** by following the simple instructions in this book."*

Amanda, Class of 2019

THE ULTIMATE LAW STUDENT GET-A-JOB CHECKLIST

A step-by-step guide to help
every student land a great job

By

Ross Fishman, JD
CEO, Fishman Marketing, Inc.

Edited by
Kerriann Stout, Esq.
Vinco Bar Exam Coaching

© 2019 Fishman Marketing, Inc. All rights reserved.

Published by Ross Fishman, Highland Park, Illinois

www.fishmanmarketing.com

ISBN: 9781792669798
Manufactured in the United States
Cover design by Michelle Benjamin

No part of this document may be reproduced or transmitted in any form by any means, electronic or mechanical, including photocopying, recording or by information storage and retrieval system, without permission from the publisher.

ADDITIONAL BOOKS BY ROSS FISHMAN

THE ULTIMATE LAW FIRM ASSOCIATE'S MARKETING CHECKLIST

The Renowned Step-By-Step, Year-By-Year Process for Lawyers Who Want to Develop Clients

THE ULTIMATE WOMEN ASSOCIATES' LEGAL MARKETING CHECKLIST

With Susan Freeman, M.A.

WE'RE SMART. WE'RE OLD. AND WE'RE THE BEST AT EVERYTHING

The World's First No-BS Guide to Legal Marketing and Branding

THE ULTIMATE PUBLIC RELATIONS HANDBOOK FOR LAWYERS

Co-Author, John Hellerman

THE ULTIMATE LAW FIRM ASSOCIATE'S MARKETING CHECKLIST (CHINESE EDITION)

Edited by Cherry Zhang, LL.M.

Available at fishmanmarketing.com and Amazon.com

amazon

Table of Contents

SECTION	PAGE
Foreword	7
Preface	11
Introduction	15
How I Got My First Job	21
You Gotta Hustle. And *Look* Like It.	25
Figure Out What You Want to Do ASAP	29
Social Media	33
Career Services	43
First-Semester	45
Second-Semester First-Years	49
Your New Goal: *Focus*	51
Target-Marketing Worksheet	59
Networking Skills	65
Write, Speak, Repurpose, and Reuse	71
So, What Should You Do at School?	75
Writing a Persuasive Resume and Cover Letter	81
Second-Year Students (2Ls)	85
Third-Year Students (3Ls)	89
General Mindset	95
Addendum	99
Author Biographies	107
Acknowledgments	111

© 2019 Fishman Marketing, Inc. All rights reserved. Do not duplicate.

Foreword

Grades are often used as a way to identify "qualified" candidates. But not all of us graduated in the top 25%. This book does a fantastic job of showing how to make yourself stand out, no matter where you rank in your class.

I love this little book. It lays out simple, practical steps to ensure your activities and experience are *different* from your competitors, and your resume will look like no other.

Your resume will have a positive narrative that grabs a hiring professional's attention and helps show exactly how you'll fit into their particular firm or organization. Further, your interviewers will clearly remember you and your unique experiences—and getting them to remember you is at least half the battle.

I've hired a lot of lawyers over the years, both laterals and law students, and it's challenging work. Look at it from the hiring side, we're asked to make important, potentially life-changing decisions based simply on whatever information gets squeezed onto a single sheet of resume paper or an online form.

We do our best but, candidly, our hiring assessments can feel pretty arbitrary, based on our "gut" and whatever "personal chemistry" we happen to feel during the artificial environment of a job interview. Trying to improve our accuracy, we rely on things we can *measure*, like GPA, law school rank, and extracurricular activities.

Deep down, we know these metrics aren't guarantees of actual success; plenty of law grads who looked good on paper quickly wash out. And we fear we're mistakenly rejecting great candidates simply because their resume didn't grab us.

Firms use GPA and other objective criteria because we're rarely given much else to go on. When one law student looks much like the next, it can be a challenge for hiring teams to even *remember* who they interviewed the day before. Very few applicants are especially memorable, and a collection of random extracurriculars don't help convey how you'll fit in.

Follow the steps laid out in this powerful little book and you'll have plenty of actual, relevant experience, and a resume that will float to the top of the pile. And that's what you need to be on your way toward a great job, and a personally fulfilling career.

Jordan Goodman
Senior Partner
Horwood Marcus & Berk, Chicago

"You won't lag behind, because you'll have the speed.
You'll pass the whole gang and you'll soon take the lead.
Wherever you fly, you'll be best of the best.
Wherever you go, you will top all the rest."

"Except when you *don't*.
Because, sometimes, you *won't*."

Oh, the Places You'll Go!
Dr. Seuss

Preface

Preface

If you're reading this book you're probably not in the top 10% of your class. Maybe law school hasn't turned out exactly how you planned. You're worried about your future. Your head's spinning, and you're wondering how you're going to land the great job you've been hoping for.

I hear you. I've been where you are.

In fact, I graduated law school in the bottom-half of my class.

But, my story has a happy ending and yours can too. Class rank be damned, I still got a great job, at a top salary, at a leading Chicago law firm. But I had to do it *my* way. I didn't simply follow the Standard Operating Procedure. Instead, I used marketing and personal-branding strategies to achieve my professional goals.

The best part? You can too, and this book will show you precisely how.

In my first attempt to secure a full-time job as a lawyer, I followed the plan recommended by the law school. I copied the straightforward "Enclosed please find my resume" cover letter and organized my resume using their standard format. Then I sent resumes to 100 different Chicago-area law firms.

Half of them never bothered responding. The other half sent form rejection letters that assured me that I had "an impressive resume and a bright future" (just not with *them*). There I was, wallowing in debt without a job to help pay for it.

If the thought of this happening to you keeps you up at night, keep reading.

After all that wasted effort, I realized I would need a different approach. If my grades were not going to interest the employers' hiring professionals, I'd need to capture their attention another way. But *how*? *That* is what this book will detail—how you can get a good-paying job and build a fulfilling career that you can be *passionate* about, doing work you love, for terrific clients.

The Ultimate Law Student Get-A-Job Checklist

I will teach you how to set yourself apart from your fellow law students and gain positive attention from leading law firms and organizations, even if your GPA isn't impressive or you're attending a lower-ranked law school. Or both.

This same personal-branding strategy will help you throughout your career, whether you're planning to open your own firm straight out of school or want to have your own clients when you're chasing partnership in a private law firm.

Start *now*. You can still have that legal career you've dreamt about. You got disappointing grades? Fine. That's not ideal, but there's still time. You need to rethink your priorities and activities. Take the long view. Spend your remaining time in law school building an impressive, attention-grabbing, job-getting resume. Only one element of that overall effort is your grade point average.

I'm going to help you create a personal brand and resume that will motivate the *right* professionals at the *right* employers to want to meet you.

It's time to look at your future. Law school grades can be a poor indicator of professional success. I've trained over 20,000 lawyers in marketing and client-development at hundreds of law firms worldwide. Many of the happiest and most-successful lawyers I know started in the bottom-half of their classes, often at lower-ranked schools.

But you need to get that first job to launch your successful career. Following the steps laid out below will help set you on the path to professional success much earlier.

Getting the most out of this book will require some introspection. I'm going to ask you to think about your personality, your skills, passions, interests, and life experience. Stop to fill in the forms where indicated; they'll help guide you to the next step or inform the tools you'll need to build to help prepare yourself for a great job and rewarding career. This book will provide the information, but you're going to need to do the personal work.

Preface

I don't want you to just get a well-paying *job*. I want you to get the *right* job, the *best* job for you, the one that will help propel you forward. I'm going to help you look five or ten years down the road, to determine how you can be more than just another skilled-but-anonymous lawyer. I want you to strive to become one of the go-to lawyers in your chosen area.

Imagine spending your career not just as a lawyer, but as a *leader*. *That* is ultimately what we want you aiming for.

Don't compete on their terms. Change the playing field. Tilt it in your direction. The remarkable part is that it's not that difficult, because most law students (and lawyers) do the same old things the same old way—we're a precedent-based bunch. In this book, I'm going to teach you how to not just *look* different but *be* different. *Better*, actually.

Rather than going down the obvious, expected path, I'm going to show you how to be focused and targeted in building your personal brand. Instead of developing a standard resume, I'm going to have you first identify your ideal career. Then you'll use personal-branding tools to create the unique and impressive experience that will intrigue and seduce the hiring professionals at select organizations.

Your reconstructed resume will show potential employers how you *are* the lawyer they've always been looking for—but didn't think existed.

You'll need to offer *more*.
Do you know how to do that?

Probably not.
But read the next few chapters and you *will*.

I wish you all the success you deserve.
Good luck!

Ross

Introduction

Introduction

The surest path to having your pick of the most-rewarding or highest-paying jobs is to excel academically and make Law Review. This is not necessarily the best indicator of long-term career success or satisfaction, but grades are the credential most hiring professionals use to evaluate your worth.

That's the game you're playing, and there are plenty of resources promising to teach you how to excel in law school. Your first-semester goal should be to work hard and earn top marks.

Unfortunately, 50% of hard-working law students will be in the bottom half of the class. That's just math. Three-quarters won't make the top quartile. For many devastated students, this will be the first time they'll have failed to succeed academically.

And *that's* the reason I wrote this book.

If you've made it this far, you have likely determined that your GPA alone isn't going to motivate prestigious law firms or agencies to woo you with lucrative job offers. That's OK, there are other paths to the top of the mountain.

You'll never forget the shattering moment you opened that envelope or email displaying your lower-than-expected GPA. Take some time to process your emotions on this. However, beginning immediately after you regain your wits, you should be laser-focused on creating the personal brand that's going to get you a great job by some other means. You have "failed" by one unit of measurement. But note that that's only one of many. You now have roughly 2-1/2 long years to methodically construct another, and that's more than enough time.

Your new goal should be to immediately undertake the activities that will best position you to land a great job anyway, albeit under different circumstances. That is, if you're not going to earn an interview with a celestial GPA, then fight your way to the top of the "Intriguing resume, let's look at this kid" pile.

Take a deep breath, you can do this. *Start now*—the more time you have ahead of you, the easier it'll be. Whether you want to work at a private law firm or government agency, or to hang out your shingle as a solo practitioner, your goal should be the same—to create a positive personal brand, reputation, and name recognition within a significant, specific, target audience.

Your likeliest new path to success is to become a specialist in a small niche industry or sub-subset of a larger industry *while still in school*, and then use this specialty to get hired by an employer that focuses on this area. You want to look like someone who can add value in ways unrelated to GPA. Your grades might not impress, but your targeted experience soon *will*.

One startling insight you'll gain after a few years in practice is that the world is full of smart, hard-working, and thoroughly *interchangeable* lawyers. Ask clients what they're looking for in a lawyer, and they'll commonly respond that they seek out those "who understand [their] business and industry." But they can rarely find them.

Any reasonably competent lawyer can learn to draft a basic lease or contract or litigate a straightforward lawsuit. You want to be the rare lawyer who can speak the clients' language, who understands their business, and offers truly useful, contextual advice and counsel. As a law student, you want to be able to show that skill to the law firms that represent those clients.

You want to be viewed as a knowledgeable, trusted industry insider, not just an eager new graduate with a scuff-free briefcase. Competing for a job within that enormous talent pool is a crapshoot; any decent law firm will receive dozens or hundreds of look-alike resumes for each available position.

Create a specialty area they can't find in every other applicant and you'll significantly increase the chance that you'll catch the eye of a savvy recruiter. To make this happen, you're going to need to spend time during law school gaining some actual real-world experience. If you look like you can hit the ground running as a lawyer, and demonstrate that your practical experience will make their lives a bit easier, then your resume will grab their eye.

I'm going to help. The tasks to get you there aren't hard. They're just hard *work*. But if you're in law school, you've already proven that you're smart and driven to succeed. I just want you to redirect some of that energy and drive toward building your future career.

If your resume looks like you've spent three years lounging around school, you have a big problem. Sure, if you're at a top-ranked school, you can study all day and night and land a great job. But that's not the case at lower-ranked schools. Those students have to work harder to prove their merit.

One Career Services professional from a lower-tier law school cuts right to it. She tells her students, "If you just sit in class for three years you won't get a job. Period." Wow. *Harsh*. But true.

You need to look like you're out there *fighting*, engaged, learning how to be a lawyer. Get some real-world experience any way you can, as soon as possible. Start early and work at it consistently throughout school.

This book is a simple, practical, and step-by-step list of precisely what activities you can undertake to avoid floundering and increase the chance that you'll get hired for your *perfect* job. Or, if not the perfect job, at least the job that will act as the launching pad to the next phase of your career.

The strategies I'm advocating in this book can help *anyone*, even the students at the *top* of the class. Just because you did well during your first semester doesn't mean you can take it easy. You never know what the rest of law school will bring and developing the skills in this book are an insurance policy.

Also, even if you're operating at a high tier, you're still competing against others across the nation who also earned top marks. Differentiation is important regardless of the nature or quality of your competition.

If you have any comments, please feel free to email them to *ross@fishmanmarketing.com*. I'd be delighted to hear from you.

As Dr. Seuss wrote in
Oh, the Places You'll Go!

> "I'm sorry to say so
> but, sadly, it's true
> that Bang-ups
> and Hang-ups
> *can happen to you.*"

Yes, they can. And apparently, they did.
But that's OK. This is just a bump in the road.
You can still have a long and successful career.

How I Got My First Job

How I Got My First Job

I'm from Chicago and attended Emory University School of Law in Atlanta. It's a top-25 school today, but at the time, it only had a regional reputation across the Southeast. Back home, I frequently heard "Emory? I thought that was a medical school."

Actually, I had earned excellent litigation credentials for a third-year law student. Emory had a remarkable and mandatory trial-advocacy training program. Every second-year Emory law student spent their two-week spring vacation in 10-hour daily classes learning how to try cases.

As a result of this trial-ad program and a summer internship at the Cook County State's Attorney's Office, I had learned basic trial skills and finished that summer having first-chaired nine felony jury trials. This is more juries than most senior partners at business law firms will see in a lifetime.

As an over-achieving law student, I won most of them. I was confident that back in Chicago this real-life experience would separate me from the pack and lead to a steady stream of job interviews.

Drafting my resume during my 3L year, I had mimicked the recommended layout: name and address at the top, followed by the name of your law school and grade point average. Below that, work experience, then activities. I was uncomfortable that this structure did not seem to highlight my particular strengths but wasn't ready to buck the system.

I thought my exceptional trial experience would be enough, but not a single law firm invited me for an interview. I suspected that they'd stopped skimming my resume after seeing my "no-name" law school and mediocre grades. They'd never even noticed all my successful jury trials.

Further, my boring cover letter simply expressed the obvious, that I was a law student seeking employment and invited them to read the resume.

It seemed that I needed a different approach. First, I re-organized and redesigned my resume to highlight my trial experience earlier, and in large, bold type. Next, I edited my cover letter to frame my capabilities and capture my readers' attention.

I reshaped my story, highlighting my jury-trial differentiators. I needed them to view me as a relatively experienced litigator, fully trained and up-to-speed, with skills far beyond those of my same-level graduating peers. I basically pitched myself as a third-year associate they could get for the price of a first-year.

I'd explained in my cover letter that because of my work interning in the criminal courts, I required less supervision and could hit the ground running better than other new law grads. I also offered some real-world criminal-defense experience which could enhance a business law firm's skillset and offer additional services they could sell to clients when a CEO's kid got a speeding ticket or arrested for a DUI.

My revised resume told a simple, clear story that the firms weren't hearing from all of my generic 3L competitors. And I didn't put the burden on them to figure out why they should hire me—I told them right up front.

With this new narrative, I distributed a second wave of resumes and got immediate and significant interest from the very firms who'd rejected me just weeks before. I started booking frequent in-person interviews with well-known law firms, snagging a job with a high-quality middle-market firm at an above-market salary. I got a better job at higher pay than most of my law school friends who had better grades.

**You Gotta Hustle.
And *Look* Like It.**

Most practicing lawyers in the US work in small firms with 2-10 lawyers. Small-firm partners complain that they "don't have time to babysit" lawyers fresh out of school. We all know that many law schools don't teach enough practical skills; you're going to need to build many of them on your own.

Small law firms have difficulty training lawyers. They don't have dedicated full-time professional-development experts helping get their new hires up-to-speed like big firms. Every minute they're spending teaching a new lawyer how to do something basic is a minute they're not making money.

As many employers remind us, their job isn't to train you. Your job is to help them make money.

Spend a minute thinking about that last paragraph; it's a critical piece of insight you'll need to bear in mind during your first five years of practice.

It's your job to get yourself trained on some of the things they need. Then your resume has to detail that for them.

Get some useful, practical experience during school. Small firms don't expect you to be able to practice law, obviously, they know you're fresh out of school. But running a small, lean business, they'd rather hire a lawyer who is partly trained and can add value. So *be* that lawyer.

During law school, find a job in a pro bono program or practical externship. Volunteer at Legal Aid or the courts, so you know something about how the system work, or how to interview clients. Get a part-time job where you can write a few basic Wills or housing contracts. Find a way to learn how to handle simple landlord-tenant issues or watch some depositions.

With a job during law school, you'll learn to schedule meetings, do research, fill in forms, make copies, and file paperwork. Now you're starting to add a little bit of value—you've become mildly useful. You've seen how the law works and proven that you're not expecting to get fed like a baby bird. It doesn't matter if it's paid or unpaid work or a school program. *Just get some experience!*

This training will separate you from the students who study hard then go home. You'll graduate with some practical insight or technical skills that someone at a small firm can benefit from. You're not a charity case. You can do things they can bill a client for. You're making them money.

Getting a law-related summer job after your first year is important.

It can be a challenge, there are few paid positions, and most law students need to earn money over the summers. But it's important to your career to get legal experience during those important 2-3 summer months.

Look at the big picture—this job is an investment in your long-term future. Find an unpaid clerkship or internship. Volunteer somewhere that gives you something to add to the top of your resume. Your long-term future may depend on it. Earn money working nights or weekends if necessary.

Figure Out What You Want to Do ASAP

Figure out what you want to do first. Then build the resume that convinces someone to hire you to do it.

Let's say you want to practice Family Law. Here's a basic list of the type of activities that can build that resume:

- Start by taking all the family law-related classes offered by your school.

- Talk to the professor who teaches those classes and find a way to be of assistance outside of class.
  - Get to know them; they can be a powerful professional resource.
  - These practice-specific professors are probably connected into the local legal community in that practice area and might have some good insight or connections to share.

- Find a way to get hired as a clerk in a small family law practice nearby one or two afternoons per week.

- Join the local bar association and the family law committee.
  - Focus your personal networking on that group.
  - Your best chance at getting a job is most likely to come via someone you meet there.
  - Work in the free family law clinic.

- Get out of school and off your couch.
  - Network, network, network.

Follow this same strategy, obviously, if you want to practice personal injury, criminal defense, estate planning, etc.

Figuring out what area of law you want to practice isn't easy. But the earlier you make this decision, the more robust and targeted your resume can become.

Employers say that they want to see "grit." They want to see law students who hustle, who take nothing for granted, and don't wait for jobs to come to them. Good lawyers have that type of persistence as well, figuring things out and getting things done. It's a trait employers will hire for.

Remember, some of these potential employers will stereotype younger-generation workers as expecting participation trophies. You can overcome that negative bias by showing that you're a hard worker, both in your resume and personal behavior.

Roughly 80% of the jobs are filled via personal relationships, not LinkedIn or Indeed.com. You must get out and meet the people who might be hiring or know someone who is. If you're someone they like and find impressive, you're immediately a lower hiring risk than an impersonal resume they receive online or from a stranger.

You must grow your network, then stay top of mind, so when one of their peers says, "Hey, I'm looking to hire a first-year lawyer, do you know anyone?" they *immediately* think of you.

If you're attending law school out of state but planning to practice back home, your local law school network won't be as helpful. You will need to build your network in your *home* legal market, so have a plan to accomplish that. This makes your summer jobs and networking-related activities even more important. See more below under Networking Skills.

Social Media

I'm going to ask you to leverage the power of social media over time to connect with your targets and build your resume. So, do it carefully, methodically, and thoughtfully. Be strategic and you'll avoid the mistakes that could inhibit your long-term success.

Before offering a candidate a job, many employers will review their social media profiles, posts, and photos, including LinkedIn, Facebook, Twitter, Instagram, and YouTube. Some states have ethics rules restricting this online stalking but, regardless, give them no ammunition they could potentially use to eliminate you from consideration.

If there's anything online you wouldn't proudly show your grandmother, *delete* it. This isn't the time to stand on principle, getting a job is too important. If it's even remotely questionable, just get rid of it.

Before you engage in any marketing efforts, review your state's ethics rules governing the use of marketing, communication, and social media generally Rules 7.1–7.4; see *http://goo.gl/JOhhF*. Frankly, there's not much a professional would want to do that's prohibited, but it's good to know the rules, just in case. Use your head.

The first step in leveraging social media for your personal brand is to create persuasive personal profiles. So, once you've selected your target specialty (that you'll identify in the "Your New Goal: Focus" chapter), create biographies on many different social platforms that you can use to highlight your commitment to this area. Detail your general skills, practical experience, and specialty industry.

You don't want to look like you're *only* interested in one particular area, just that you're much more interested and experienced in that area than your peers.

LinkedIn

Did you know that there are nearly 600 million people using LinkedIn every day for networking? It is the most-important social media tool for young professionals, the one preferred by lawyers. It hasn't quite taken off as a communication platform, but it's the foundation of most professionals' personal marketing. It's where you'll post articles and updates to your growing network.

Today, nearly everyone you would want to hire you, from Hiring Partner to client, will first skim your LinkedIn profile to learn more about you. So, make it persuasive, personal, and professional. Show them that you're more than a dispassionate one-page resume. This is your opportunity to help your targets see how wonderful you are and how lucky they'd be to have you on their team.

- ❑ If you don't have a LinkedIn page, create one.
  - Draft a detailed LinkedIn personal profile.
  - Infuse it with your vibrant personality.
  - Ensure there are no typos. Zero. None.
    - A single typo could be disqualifying.
    - Have a friend proofread it for you.

- ❑ Build a sizable LinkedIn network, work toward hundreds of connections.
  - Start by connecting with people you know personally such as family, friends, peers, acquaintances, and classmates from all your schools.
  - Your goal is to get to 500 connections as soon as possible. Once you hit 500 connections, LinkedIn just shows "500+" on your profile. This works as social proof to others that you have an established professional network.
    - Join your law school LinkedIn group, and connect with anyone you know.
    - Consider starting a group for your graduation class.
  - Once you have a complete profile and established network you can start reaching out and connecting with professors, speakers you've heard at events, individuals who work at firms you are interested in, *etc.* Please feel free to connect with me as well.

Social Media

- ☐ Fill it out completely, including the Contact Information and Education sections.
    - The two most-important areas are Summary and Experience.
    - The Summary section is the very first thing people will read after your name and headline.
    - The Experience section is where you get the opportunity to highlight all the exciting ways you have built up your personal brand, professional experience, and target niche (that I will be teaching you to do in the following chapters)
    - Read the "How to Write a LinkedIn Profile" form in the Addendum.

- ☐ Add a quality photograph.
    - An inexpensive passport photo from Walgreens will suffice.
        - You should dress similar to how you would look at a professional networking event.
        - Smile. Look like someone they might want to work with.
    - No cropped vacation, party, wedding, or group photos.
        - Nothing cute, grainy, badly lit, far away, or blurry. No pets or props. Be smart.

- ☐ If you have an existing LinkedIn page, do a thorough audit to ensure it is highly professional.
    - Delete anything the most-conservative grey-haired employer could possibly find offensive.
    - Be judicious in what you include.
        - Delete all items from high school.
        - Be sensible regarding college activities.
    - Write in the first person and use a friendly, casual tone.
    - Create a custom public profile URL, so it's not random letters and numbers.
        - Find an explainer video online that details the simple steps.
    - Review the privacy settings for your profile. You want your profile to be Public so that people can see and connect with you. However, it is important to keep in mind that anything you "like" or "comment" on will be visible to anyone in your network, so use discretion.

The Ultimate Law Student Get-A-Job Checklist

- ☐ Like, join, or follow professional groups within your chosen specialty area.
  - ○ Show your commitment to this industry or practice.

- ☐ Post occasional relevant updates, including thought-leadership pieces you will be writing in your chosen area of specialization/focus.

- ☐ It's easy to start by sharing or liking things that others in your specialty area have posted.
  - ○ This will also visibly reinforce your commitment to this area.
  - ○ Remember, listening and engaging with what others post is as important, if not more important, in social networking as what *you* say and post.

- ☐ No one expects your profile to be very long; just write simply and proficiently.

- ☐ Update it regularly, *at least* every few months, especially when your career is developing.
  - ○ Ideally you should update it every time you publish an article, give a presentation, join a new committee, etc.
  - ○ Check it at least weekly.

- ☐ Regularly "Endorse" classmates, friends, and peers; it only takes a *click*. They'll typically endorse you back.
  - ○ Create evidence that you are well-liked, a leader among your group.
  - ○ A word of caution with Skills and Endorsements: When you receive an endorsement from someone for a specific skill, only post it on your bio if you have actual expertise in that area. Some state bar rules have restrictions on this.
    - When in doubt, leave it off.

- ☐ Note that anyone whose LinkedIn profile you visit will receive a notification that you'd been there.
  - ○ You can turn this off and browse in Stealth Mode.
  - ○ There are simple explainer videos on this topic.

twitter

Twitter is a simple, quick, efficient platform to connect yourself to your specialty area online. Just 280 characters including spaces—a couple casual sentences and hashtags. It is an ideal communications platform to help build your brand and contact with others in a specialty area or industry niche.

- ❑ If you don't have a Twitter account, create one under your name.
    - ○ For example, I'm @rossfishman.
    - ○ Check it occasionally.

- ❑ Build your Twitter network; connect with your peers, professors, industry contacts, and thought leaders.
    - ○ Follow people, companies, associations, and organizations within your legal, business, and specialty niche areas of interest.

- ❑ Post weekly on something relating to your chosen specialty area.
    - ○ Remember to include the narrow search engine optimized (SEO) keywords that the media and experts in this industry or area would use to search.
    - ○ Ensure you learn the nuances of the jargon.
    - ○ Posts with photos or graphics get significantly greater attention.

- ❑ Re-tweet the tweets that resonate with you, to help grow your network.

- ❑ Consider utilizing Twitter as a *listening* platform to better understand your specialty area, scholars, and more.
    - ○ Pay attention to what they are promoting, discussing, and commenting on. It can all be valuable.

facebook

Consider Facebook to be a defensive strategy. You're unlikely to positively influence decision-makers using your personal Facebook profile, but an unfortunate post or photo could eliminate you from consideration. Don't risk it.

- ❏ Analyze your Facebook page. Do a detailed audit to sanitize it.
  - Upgrade your privacy security settings to hide yourself from prying eyes.
  - Delete any party photos, *etc.*
  - Delete anything a conservative senior partner could possibly find offensive.
    - If you wouldn't proudly show it to your grandmother, *delete* it.
  - Keep it casual and sensible. This is a less-formal medium than LinkedIn.
  - Consider creating a new public Facebook page as a platform to support the professional brand you're creating.
    - Add occasional updates and photos of your specialty events, speeches, meetings, etc.
    - You can post similar content here that you would post on LinkedIn.

Instagram

As with Facebook, you will want to use a defensive strategy with Instagram. Instagram isn't the place your target audience will visit for professional marketing, but your personal profile may show up in a basic search of your name.

- ❏ Analyze your Instagram profile. Do a detailed audit to sanitize it.
  - Consider making your profile private or change your Instagram name.
  - Delete any party photos, *etc.*
  - Delete anything a conservative senior partner could possibly find offensive.
    - If you wouldn't proudly show it to your grandmother, *delete* it.

YouTube is the second most frequently used search engine. If you have a YouTube account, analyze it carefully for any videos that do not support your professional strategy.

- ❏ Hide, delete, or mark "Private" any videos that do not exemplify the type of persona you are trying to create.

- ❏ Be careful with any videos you like or comment on and what channels you follow because this could be visible to others as well.

- ❏ Create a new YouTube account for the short specialty videos you may soon be creating.

- ❏ You can shoot high-definition videos with your smartphone.
  - ○ Buy an inexpensive tabletop tripod and spring-clip smartphone holder. You can find them online for $10.

- ❏ Review the "Write, Speak, Repurpose, and Reuse" chapter below for ideas.

Snapchat

Snapchat won't help you professionally, but it can hurt you. As with the other forms of social media, use good judgment about the content you create and share. You never know who is watching.

Business Cards

- ☐ *Always* have business cards with you.

- ☐ They may seem old-fashioned to some, but they remain a vital part of today's networking, particularly with the older people who can hire you.
  - ○ A quality card looks professional, and you want to be ready whenever you meet someone who could turn into a valuable lead or connection.

- ☐ Cards remain the simplest, most tangible way for people to remember you and contact you later.

- ☐ Include your name, email address, cell phone, LinkedIn profile URL, Twitter username/handle (including the @ sign), law school name, and expected graduation date.
  - ○ Add "Law Student" as your job title.

- ☐ Consider adding more detail regarding your chosen specialty, e.g. "Law student focused on aviation law."

- ☐ Go online and order 250 cards on smooth, bright-white, 110-pound card stock.
  - ○ We like Overnightprints.com or Vistaprint.com for fast, inexpensive, digital printing.

- ☐ Don't leave these business cards to gather dust in your bottom drawer; they can't help you unless they're with you. Here's how to guarantee you have cards when you need them:
  - ○ Leave 75–100 in the box in your desk, then divide up the rest among all of your pants pockets, suit coats, blazers, jackets, overcoats, purses, gym bags, briefcase, backpack, suitcase, roller bag, and glove box.
  - ○ Put a rubber-banded stack in your suitcase, so you don't forget them when you're traveling.
  - ○ Watch this brief video about business cards. *https://youtu.be/rAA3291QWnQ.*

- ❏ Women's outfits may not have pockets.
    - ○ Plan for networking events by wearing a blazer with pockets.
    - ○ Ensure you have a purse with a shoulder strap and keep your cards in an outside pocket, so you can effortlessly pull them out with one hand.
    - ○ In a pinch, you can insert a few cards in the back of your plastic name tag, or in your cell phone case.

- ❏ At networking events, to avoid embarrassing mix-ups, always keep your own cards in your *left*-side pants or jacket pockets, and the cards you collect on your *right* side.

Career Services

Career Services

You're going to need to take personal responsibility for your job search, which means using all the resources that are available to you. Among the most under-utilized resources is right down the hall—your school's Career Services professionals. These people are dedicated to your success. It's their *job* to help you find a job.

Sure, helping law review students get high-paying jobs at prestigious firms makes them look good. But they're also being evaluated based upon how many total graduating students get law-related jobs within a year of graduation.

That is, many law school-ranking services are using entirely new metrics to evaluate the quality of the nation's schools. Instead of simply measuring the college GPA or LSAT score of the incoming first-year class, influential rankings like AboveTheLaw.com are looking at the percentage of a law school's grads who are getting legal jobs. There's increasing pressure on schools to help all of their students find jobs, and they have sophisticated tools to help you. I'll be asking you to conduct your own internet research to find particular lawyers and firms who specialize in the target areas you've selected. But most Career Services departments have searchable resources and databases that can help you find these potential employers as well. They can help you identify the practice area and specialties of particular law firms and organizations.

As I mentioned previously, I've spoken with countless Career Services professionals who are frustrated that they don't get to help as many students as they would like. You must seek their assistance; they can't come to you. They sincerely want to help you succeed. And one plea I hear regularly is to stay in touch and keep them updated about your job search. Answer their calls and emails! Law schools today are being ranked on post-graduation employment data to comply with the ABA accreditation standards and provide meaningful statistics to *US News* and other rating platforms.

Accurate reporting is important, and the more information they have about who got hired, when, and where, the better your school may do in the rankings. You want your law school to continue rising in the rankings, so help them out—let them know when you get hired. They'll celebrate your exciting news and accomplishment with you.

First-Semester

First-Years (1Ls)

MINDSET:

Work hard. Get on Law Review.

Your first priority is to try to be a great law student; who knows, you might find yourself in the top 25%. During this time, your only real proactive, external activity should be ensuring that you don't lose contact with the people you already know.

Maintain relationships with friends from college, and keep up with your hobbies and any worthwhile organizations you belong to. It's easy to get so caught up in law school that the outside world fades away. Create reminders to ensure you maintain some contact with your buddies every few months. Your future self will thank you.

Build your personal brand within your law school. Immediately concentrate on internal marketing by developing relationships with your peers in your class and the other sections, as well as professors, administrators, and Career Services professionals. Work to gain visibility and name recognition; your peers will become your first lawyer network and later may turn into referral sources and clients if they get jobs in-house.

The better you look, the better you compete.

The differentiation strategies you'll learn in this book are the same ones that top rainmakers use to get clients as senior partners. The professional network you'll be building during school can become your clients later. No effort is wasted, take the long view.

Here's how to begin the battle to create your brightest future:

- ❑ Keep in touch with your existing personal network, leveraging both traditional and online tools.
    - ○ Go to events, send holiday cards, schedule breakfasts, lunches, or drinks.
    - ○ Stay visible on social media, e.g., LinkedIn, Facebook, Twitter, Instagram, Snapchat, etc.
- ❑ Get to know your school's Careers Services professionals; they can be a great resource, and most of them sincerely care about their students.

The Ultimate Law Student Get-A-Job Checklist

- o They often have valuable career opportunities to share. If they see that you are diligently working at getting hired they're in a better position to help you achieve your goals.
- o Many Career Services pros say that the students who need their assistance the most, seek it the least.
  - Don't make that mistake, go get some help. Start early!

☐ Grow your network. Create a mailing list or e-mail list spreadsheet of friends and contacts.
- o There is free software out there such as MailChimp that can help you manage this information.
- o Opt for more, rather than fewer people, when deciding whom to add.

☐ Before you add anyone to an email list where you will be sending mass emails, make sure that you have their permission to do so.
- o Law school classmates
- o Childhood, high school, and college friends
- o Former colleagues from previous jobs
- o Community association and professional club contacts
- o People you'll meet in your specialty area

☐ If you don't have a Gmail email address, create one.
- o Your law school email account will likely disappear shortly after graduation, do not use it for job-hunting purposes.
- o Avoid AOL, Hotmail, Yahoo!, Zoho, or other free email services. Gmail is the standard for personal email accounts. You'll need it for the future, even after you have one with a law firm domain.
- o An Outlook.com email address would be the next best option; you may continue using that. But if you're starting fresh, go with Gmail.

☐ Your Gmail account should look professional, using your first and last names—no adjectives or cute nicknames. Use your middle initial if necessary, or numbers afterwards if your name is already taken.

☐ Check your email at least once every day, including weekends.
- o Someone important may try to reach you at odd hours, and it is important to show responsiveness.

Second-Semester First-Years

MINDSET:

If your grades won't impress top law firms, build something else that will.

This is the time you should create the basic platform you'll be working from over the next few years, the specific infrastructure you'll gradually expand through graduation and well into practice.

Look around at your classmates. Some are building their resume for leadership, as Class President, Social Chair, or other social accolades. That can be useful as it sets them apart from the rest of the class in a positive way.

I want you to aspire to do even *more*.

More than generic "Leadership," seek to work toward leadership in an area that offers a specific type of specialty or industry expertise. Class President is basically a popularity contest, or at least a battle of name recognition. That's considered valuable, it shows future employers that your peers like or respect you.

But with limited additional effort, you can make yourself valuable to the people who *really* matter, the Hiring Partners or other recruiting professionals. You just need to show them exactly *how* you're uniquely valuable to their particular firm or organization.

If you're likely to work in a small firm, get involved in at least one student group—in a meaningful way.

No one cares about what groups you've simply "joined" if you haven't held a significant leadership position or been in charge of something you can discuss in an interview. But only join *one* student group, it's more important to have actual legal experience of some sort. Don't spread yourself too thin. Be sure to connect your student group to your career interest.

Think about a practice area-specific group, like a criminal defense, personal injury, or energy group. Consider volunteering for the school's pro bono efforts or legal clinic in an area supporting your preferred area, like family law or immigration.

Your New Goal: *Focus*

"You have brains in your head.
You have feet in your shoes.
You can steer yourself any direction you choose."

"You're on your own. And you know what you know.
And *YOU* are the guy who'll decide where to go."

Oh, the Places You'll Go!
Dr. Seuss

It's time to decide where you want your career to go.

Here's the main point: Regardless of the situation, you never want to be just another smart and skilled but generic applicant. You want to be the one who offers *more*—a particular skill or expertise that doesn't also exist in precisely that same quantity in every other student in your graduating class.

I want you to concentrate your efforts more narrowly, particularly toward an industry group or sub-specialty practice niche. (See the videos at *https://goo.gl/fKR7AA* and *https://goo.gl/QtmJTT*.)

For example, I know a lot about Industrial Tire Manufacturing. My father and grandfather designed and built tires for heavy equipment, like underground mining drills, crawlers, and loaders. Growing up, tire-fill composition was typical dinner conversation.

As a child, I played with miniature Caterpillar forklifts and vulcanized rubber for my fifth-grade science-fair project. I've flown on the Goodyear blimp. I worked summers in the sooty factory in high school—sneezing oily carbon black out of my sinuses for weeks afterwards. It's the family business; my sisters know this stuff too.

That is to say, I take for granted an insider's nuanced understanding of this narrow little billion-dollar industry, full of companies like Goodyear, Goodrich, John Deere, the rubber importers, chemical manufacturers, and coal and other mining companies. *And all of those companies have law firms that provide them with regular legal advice.* I'm confident that I knew more about this industry than any law student in the country, probably more than nearly any practicing lawyer too.

Unfortunately, it never occurred to me that these types of companies would have found my unique knowledge to be valuable, or that many of the law firms representing these types of companies would have wanted to meet a law student who could speak their clients' language.

I offered expert industry insight even the most experienced partners couldn't possibly possess. I would have been a tremendous asset to the partners on new-business trips. If I'd thought to mention it, I could have stood out in a very positive and client-oriented way.

Firms all over the nation have practices that could have benefited from my expertise. Many law firms in California, Colorado, Utah, and elsewhere have practice groups representing hard-rock mines. All of the major law firms in West Virginia have dedicated coal-mining practice groups, but very few of the lawyers have actually taken a rickety elevator down into a mine. *I have.*

These mining-related industries require the full range of business and litigation legal services, including real estate, tax, environmental, labor and employment, immigration, litigation, and more. I'm not an environmental lawyer, but I'm aware of the basic regulatory issues that mines confront from the inside.

I should have been marketing my tire-industry expertise to the law firms representing the sizable industrial tire, rubber, and mining companies. Today, you can identify those firms with a simple Google search.

Additionally, most Career Services departments have databases that can help with this information. Later, as a litigation associate, instead of marketing "general commercial litigation" to Chicago-area businesses, I should have been marketing myself to companies in those particular industries.

I didn't capitalize on my experience, but *you* can. To do this, start with the industry sectors where you might have had previous job experience, e.g. real estate, construction, health care, financial services, or insurance. Did you have a family business? A job before law school? What was your college degree?

Do you have any unique hobbies or special interests? Consult the "Niche Marketing" checklist in the Addendum for more ideas. You can generate some ideas by browsing through the list of Standard Industrial Classification (SIC) codes at *https://siccode.com/en/siccode/list/directory.*

The threshold question is—what do you know that other potential hires don't, that would benefit the firms you would like to apply to?

Almost any kind of industry expertise can be helpful. My friend Steve Borkan has a specialty in defending the police and local municipalities, particularly in Taser-related cases. Another friend, Dean Gerber, specializes not in general corporate finance like tens of thousands of other lawyers, but specifically in *aviation* finance, i.e. leasing airplanes and helicopters.

We have worked with hundreds of lawyers who have developed truly unique specialty practice. These include:

- Bridge and tunnel construction in Florida
- Farms and agriculture in Central California
- Forestry regulatory in upstate New York
- Iranian divorce cases in Vancouver
- Oil and gas companies in Louisiana
- The "adult novelty" industry in California
- The beer industry, nationwide
- Divorces for horse owners
- The pest-control industry in Alabama
- DUI-defense of truck drivers in British Columbia
- Surfing law in California

If your area of expertise has a Standard Industry Classification (SIC) code, there are assuredly specialized law firms or practices whose clients would benefit if they had an associate with an insider's knowledge of that industry.

Other considerations to help identify the specialty niche or industry to target include:

- What hobby, passion, or special skill or interest of yours would firms value?
- What's hanging on your walls or sitting on your coffee table?
- What do you do in your free time, on nights and weekends?
- Where do you, your family, or spouse have an established network?
- Think through your list of friends and family members. Are several of them in one particular industry or niche?

The Ultimate Law Student Get-A-Job Checklist

Take some time to review and fill out the "Target Marketing Worksheet" form below. It is a good start toward helping you identify the particular specialty niche around which you can build a persuasive job-seeking resume and fulfilling career.

Select Your Target Group

Once you have narrowed your focus, the next step is to select the organization or association that represents that industry. Your ultimate goal is to become an involved member in that group—a highly visible, friendly, helpful, active contributor. Learn the industry and the association members. To make the most out of your membership try these tips:

- Your goal is simply to meet people, make friends, and become a valuable member of the community.

- Attend at least 8 out of 12 monthly local chapter meetings per year. I know this seems like a lot of time away from studying, but it's an important investment in your future.

- Network regularly and actively; get to know everyone. You'll find that as a law student, people will be interested in you.

- Keep the conversations focused on *them*.
    - Remember the 80/20 Rule of Communication: You should spend just 20% of the time talking, mostly asking interested, insightful questions about them and their businesses, and 80% of the time listening.
    - Remarkably, studies show that the more *they* talk, (1) the smarter they think you *are*, and (2) the more they like you!

- In all of your networking, remember, as a friend of mine once said, "It's better to be interested than to be interesting." Be actively interested in them and in facilitating their success more than being the center of attention.

- Just because the stereotypic rainmakers are gregarious doesn't mean that's why they get hired. Being outgoing helps grow their network, but they get hired because they are good at listening and finding ways to help people solve their problems. That's something anyone can do. And we generally prefer helping people to bragging about ourselves anyway.

The Ultimate Law Student Get-A-Job Checklist

- ❏ Join a committee and follow through on any assignments or responsibilities.
  - People will judge your legal skills based upon how you perform as a volunteer.
  - Do you meet your deadlines and commitments?

- ❏ If you are a member of a relevant outside organization, invite one or more of the members you meet to come speak at your school or host a panel.

Target-Marketing Worksheet

Target-Marketing Worksheet

At this point, you may be thinking, "Fine, but where should *I* focus *my* efforts?"

The goal is to identify one or more narrow niches which you could use to capture the attention of a hiring professional enough to bring you in for an interview. The long-term goal is to use this same specialty area to become a market leader in your legal practice as well.

This form is intended to help focus your thoughts regarding where you might want to start. This is really important—if you're thoughtful about your decision, the niche you choose could help you land that first job now, and a bunch of great clients later.

As discussed above, consider specific industries, narrow market segments, target communities, sub-practice specialties, and/or areas of narrow expertise. The largest and most-obvious industries in business law firms include Health Care, Real Estate, Insurance, Construction, and Banking/Financial Services.

In what area do you have the beginning of some level of expertise? Note that the smaller or more obscure the industry, the more distinctive you become, but simultaneously shrink the pool of target law firms as well. Nearly every business law firm has a real estate group, but few have a specialty in janitorial, freight trucking, or logistics services. There are more available positions in law firm Financial Services departments, but also more law students who have previously worked in banking to compete against.

There might not be many law firms that represent significant numbers of speech therapists, auto dealerships, restaurants, dentists, or printing companies, but those who do would favor the rare law student whose expertise in these areas they could leverage.

When I helped build an Alabama law firm's Pest Control Group (creatively named "The Bug Lawyers" for public relations purposes), they were anxious to hire associates who had related industry experience or a college degree in entomology.

What industry or niche specialty practice should you focus on?

Select companies that are appropriate to the size of the firm you are targeting. Larger law firms require larger companies that can pay higher hourly rates. Smaller firms more commonly represent smaller companies. The more "fun" industries are harder to break into because the competition is much greater, like sports, arts, entertainment, music, fashion, *etc*.

What skills, interest, or passion leads to an appropriate target?

What do you already know that every other law student doesn't also know precisely as well? What industry would you be interested in immersing yourself in? Try to be practical, critical, and realistic. This may require some personal introspection.

Consider:

- What industries do you particularly enjoy?

- What type of people do you have good chemistry with?
  - Do they tend to gravitate toward particular areas or industries?

- Is there something particularly interesting or unusual about you that would provide a place to start, for example:
  - Does a previous job or career provide insight?
  - What was your college major?
  - Did you work in a family business?
  - Does your spouse have a business with a good personal network?
  - Do you have any personal connections that could give you a leg up?
  - What hobby might provide useful insight?
  - Do you have other relevant experience that could get you started?

Target-Marketing Worksheet

Select *one* industry group or trade association.

Often the answer isn't obvious. So, to help you identify your narrow niche, visit a public or law library and review a print copy of Gale Publishing's multi-volume *Encyclopedia of Associations*. It can be helpful (and surprisingly fun) to simply skim through the volume containing the alphabetical list of associations. You are likely to find areas that would never have initially occurred to you.

- ❏ Browse through the easy-to-use 25,000-association directory to identify possible industries or areas of focus, and the best trade groups or professional associations related to them.
  - Seek a 500- to 1,000-member national association with an active local chapter.
  - Surround yourself with people whom you can turn into valued contacts, employers, or clients later on in your career.

- ❏ Contact the most-relevant associations to learn more about their members and request membership information.

- ❏ If the member profile sounds like a good fit, consider joining the group.
  - Validate the choice of that group with your contacts who might know it.

- ❏ Don't worry if the members are junior or mid-level professionals. Build relationships with them when you're both starting your careers. They'll be in a position to hire lawyers later, when you're in a position to get hired.

Then what?

- ❏ Get involved in the association and be an active, helpful member of the community.
  - Attend the monthly meetings.
  - Have fun, be yourself.

- ❏ Gradually work to a leadership position.
  - Committee chair
  - Membership committee

- ☐ Work to consistently increase your profile and visibility.
- ☐ Focus most of your networking activities on this group.
- ☐ Capitalize on any opportunities that arise to write short articles or give presentations.

Summary

Focusing your marketing clarifies your message and identifies how to use the standard tools most efficiently and effectively:

- ☐ Blog
    - Consider creating a simple, free WordPress blog to showcase your industry efforts. It needn't be especially robust.
    - Implicitly, simply *having* a blog proves your commitment, credibility, and credentials.

- ☐ Networking
    - Get to know the members of this community.

- ☐ Research
    - Learn about this industry. You want to be able to speak their language like an insider.
    - You can't claim to be an expert then get the jargon wrong.

- ☐ Biography
    - Add this specialty area to all of your online profiles and biographies.

- ☐ Social media
    - Add this specialty area to your LinkedIn Summary and Experience sections.
    - Tweet occasionally about this industry and your activities. Twitter doesn't take much time, and can establish or reinforce your expertise, particularly with the media.
    - Write and post updates and articles across your social media platforms like LinkedIn and Facebook.

Target-Marketing Worksheet

- ❏ Speeches, Newsletters
  - ○ Present on a narrow topic at your law school, during lunch or after school.
  - ○ The size of the audience doesn't matter.
  - ○ Submit articles for publication in newsletters.

- ❏ Law School Group
  - ○ Create your own law school group or committee, e.g. you're the Founder and President of the "Emory Pest Control-Law Group."
  - ○ Host occasional events.
  - ○ Leverage social media to spread the word.
  - ○ Learn more in the next chapter.

Networking Skills

Once you've identified your target audience and the organizations they belong to or the seminars they attend, it's time to mix and mingle with them. The obvious next question is, "So what do I do once I get there?" Let's address that directly.

Note that it doesn't really matter if a program's speaker or topic interests you. If your target audience will be there, it's probably a good idea for you to be there too. Then, once there, you must maximize your time to efficiently reinforce existing relationships and initiate new ones.

Your goal at events is to meet people in your chosen field and expand your personal network. You need to use this organization to enhance your knowledge and build your industry credibility, to create more items you can add to your resume and discussion points for job interviews.

- ❑ Networking is a *long-term* process. Learn to meet more of the *right* people, those whom you can turn into employers, prospects, business contacts, and clients.
    - ○ "Active listening" is important.
    - ○ Ask well-informed questions regarding their business.
    - ○ Listen for opportunities and ways to help them achieve their goals.
    - ○ Ask your school to bring in training on networking skills. See the brief video at *https://goo.gl/Bwq9ii*.
    - ○ Networking is a learned skill. It's not difficult, but many behaviors seem counter-intuitive.
    - ○ Most importantly, remember that the best information is gleaned by listening, not talking.

- ❑ Before the Event
    - ○ Determine whether the event you'll be attending is *business* or *social*.
        - • If it's *social*, great, have fun. But if it's *business*, then treat it like business.
        - • Be intentional and strategic. This means that invariably you'll have less fun.
    - ○ Write down a few simple, tangible goals to complete. They can be simple, e.g. "Meet two new people," or "Collect three

The Ultimate Law Student Get-A-Job Checklist

      business cards," or "Speak with Amanda at ABC Company."
- Identifying specific goals makes your behavior more strategic and intentional; it'll guide your movements and let you know if you've been successful.
- One goal should be to speak with an existing contact you know will be there. Ask two questions:
  - "How's business?" and
  - "What are you working on that you find especially interesting?"
- When blocking off the event on your calendar, block off an additional hour beyond the scheduled time.
- Commit to arriving 30 minutes before the program starts and staying 30 minutes later.
  - *That's* when the actual networking occurs, not during the presentation.
- Consider doing some quick internet research regarding any targets or prospects who you expect to be at the event.
  - Research can help provide an easy conversation starter. "Hey, I saw that you were [doing X]. Tell me about that!"
  - It also positions you as the type of informed, educated professional they should want to work with.

❏ *During* the Event
- Be strategic regarding whom you speak to. You're busy and you have taken valuable time away from school to be here.
- You have only 30 minutes to meet and speak with the people you need to help advance your career. You can't afford to risk spending this time with the "wrong" people.
- Subtly read their name tag and assess whether they fit your strategic profile *before* approaching and engaging them in conversation. (Don't get caught doing it.)
  - It might feel a tad mercenary, but remember, you've decided that this is business.
  - You're at this event to meet new people who might turn into prospects and employers, not to make friends. That's for some other time or event.
- Don't sit at empty tables. The same rule applies to where you sit—be deliberate regarding whom you'll spend lunch with.
- Choose your seatmates carefully, intentionally, and subtly.

- You'll spend an important hour between these two people. Make sure they're the "right" people for this occasion.
- Try to meet more, rather than fewer people.

❏ Wear a name tag
  - If you need to write your own, make it neat, large, and legible. It helps attendees ask you questions and remember you later.
  - Affix name tags to your *right* lapel, not your left. This way it faces towards people when shaking hands with them.
  - Women may need to plan ahead regarding their fashion choices, to avoid damaging fragile clothing with a name tag's sticker or alligator clip.
    - Have a selection of indestructible "conference blazers."
  - If you're given a lanyard, position it above your chest, so people can comfortably see it.
    - It may have a spring-clip to resize it. Tie a knot if necessary.
    - A name tag dangling around your stomach is entirely invisible. Don't make it difficult, or worse uncomfortable, for others to read your name tag.
  - When you next receive a magnetic-clip name tag, consider keeping it in your briefcase or backpack. They're the most-flexible and least-destructive style and can be reused in future events.

❏ Graceful Exit. Once you've made a good impression with someone within your target audience, create a relevant follow-up meeting or activity, commit to that follow-up, then exit the conversation so you both can continue networking.
  - To exit a conversation, it's socially acceptable to suggest that you need to make a call, use the restroom, say hello to someone you see across the room, or get a drink.
    - A friend of mine always orders a half-glass of beer at the bar. This way, he's never more than a few ounces away from an excuse to get out of an unhelpful conversation. *Clever.*
  - "I don't want to take up all your time. "I'd like to continue our conversation, so how about we plan to get together? I'll email you in the next couple days."

- Then be sure that you *do* it. Follow-up is hard. But it works.
  - Write yourself a reminder on the person's business card, detailing the promised follow-up.
    - Or write yourself a calendar reminder on your smartphone.
  - You must *force* yourself to keep moving. It's too easy to simply continue a positive conversation when things are going well.
  - Don't monopolize their networking; they probably want to speak with more people too.
  - Fight the urge to speak only to your friends. Hanging out with them is easy and fun, but that's not why you're at this event.
    - If you're uncomfortable attending events alone, go with a friend, but agree to separate at the door and not speak with each other until it's time to leave, or you're likely to spend your time hanging out with them instead of meeting new people.
    - Remember, you decided that this event would be *business*, not social.

- ❑ *After* the Event
  - Connect with the people you meet on LinkedIn within 24 hours, with a brief personal note that reminds them of who you are.
  - Add them to your contact list for appropriate mailings, holiday cards, etc.
  - Try to send a follow-up email by the next afternoon. Keep it simple and to the point, such as, "Nice meeting you, let's continue our conversation over lunch."
    - Offer a specific date, time and place in your email. Don't waste time with endless noncommittal back-and-forth communications.
    - Be polite and assertive; they will appreciate your being direct.
  - Follow up as promised. For example, you might say, "After we spoke, I looked into [the topic in question] regarding our conversation. I have attached a couple of ideas I had on this issue. Would you like to discuss them after work one day next week?"

Networking Skills

- ❏ Networking Questions. It can be difficult to get started in conversation with a stranger. Try some of these.
    - [Look at their name tag.] Tell me about [company].
    - What do you do there?
    - What kinds of products/services do you provide?
    - Who are your target customers?
    - How did you get started in _____?
    - What do you enjoy most about what you do/the topic of the event?
    - What changes do you see in the industry?
    - What are some of the projects you are currently working on?
    - What can I do to help you/your business?

Write, Speak, Repurpose, and Reuse

Creating and reusing content to spread your message across the internet

- ❏ People perceive public speaking as demonstrating real expertise.

- ❏ It is an excellent way to generate the content that you can reuse on multiple platforms, cutting it up into smaller chunks and dispersing it across the internet.

- ❏ Present a speech to your law school committee or other group. Carefully select the topic, using it to support your chosen niche or specialty practice.
  - It needn't be long; 10 minutes is plenty.
  - Your goal should be to simply give a nice, informative speech that shows that you know something about the content and industry.
  - As mentioned above, it doesn't matter how many are in the audience. The *existence* of the speech is what's most important.
    - See the video at https://goo.gl/gf9eHF.
    - Rehearse, rehearse, rehearse. Make sure you deliver it well. Treat it like a class assignment.

- ❏ With a video camera and tripod, videotape your presentation.
  - Your school's audio-visual department likely has this equipment available to borrow.
  - You can also record with your smartphone video and a small tripod with a spring-clip phone holder you can buy online for $10.
  - Upload the entire speech to Vimeo.com.
  - Trim the speech into as many quality 2- to 3-minute snippets as possible, and upload each of them to YouTube as individual videos, once every couple weeks.
    - You just created an entire YouTube channel on your chosen topic!
  - Use narrow, detailed keywords and buzzwords in the captions, tags, and descriptions so Google will index them thoroughly.

The Ultimate Law Student Get-A-Job Checklist

- ❑ Audiotape and transcribe the speech or use a free voice-to-text software to do so, e.g. the free Dragon Dictation app or Google Docs, see *https://is.gd/2ODy5J*.
  - ○ This single transcribed speech can be repurposed into *many* different-length articles and blog posts for various audiences.
  - ○ Edit the transcription into numerous tweets and social media updates.
    - The text from a single brief speech can be cut into dozens of individual tweets.
  - ○ Professional editors can do much of this work for you, if you can muster a small budget.
    - Find inexpensive freelance editors at online sites like UpWork.com or Fiverr.com.
    - "Here's the transcription of my speech and my slides. Please edit this into 25 tweets, 5 blog posts, two 1,250-word articles, and three 500-word articles."

- ❑ Upload your PowerPoint slides to slideshare.net.
  - ○ Google highly ranks SlideShare profiles.
  - ○ Create a detailed SlideShare profile.
  - ○ Use the specialized keywords of your chosen industry in the PPT's title and description.
  - ○ Link the SlideShare slides to your LinkedIn profile.

- ❑ Post links and updates of your videos and slides to Twitter, LinkedIn, Facebook, and other social media accounts.

So, What Should You Do at School?

We want you to use your limited available time, the school's Career Services resources, and the power of the internet to create a resume that makes you look like an expert in the field in which you want a job. You're showing perseverance and grit, while getting some legal experience by working occasionally after school at a small firm or volunteering at a clinic.

You're involved in a student and a professional group to build expertise in an area you're hoping to practice in. You probably won't be an *actual* substantive expert yet, but if you systematically dedicate a reasonable amount of time to the pursuit, you're going to know a lot more than your law school competitors, and your extensive resume will reflect that.

You want to create the perception of someone who is deeply committed to the particular area or industry that would benefit the firm and its clients.

For example, let's say your family business was tire manufacturing and you determined that *this* would be the specialty area you would use to help seek a law firm position. Your goal is to create as many credible items and activities as possible that you can add to your resume and post them online where they can be found with a Google search.

Think of it this way—

What would the resume of someone deeply dedicated to your chosen field look like?

- Subtract your *current* resume from *that* resume.

- Whatever is remaining, you must *create*.
  - Remember, you have 2-1/2 years or so to do this. That's plenty of time.
  - Slow and steady.
    - One line-item at a time.
    - Start small.
    - Do the simple, quick things first.

What are the easiest, fastest things to do? What's free? *Start there.*

This is not intended to be a mandatory or all-inclusive list, just some ideas. You certainly don't need to do all of them and I'm sure I've missed a number of great ideas. Just be proactive, intentional, and consistent. This is a marathon, not a sprint, you have time to build it. But never let the perfect be the enemy of the good. Get started.

More activity is better than less. You can't do it in your available "free" time, law students don't have any. You must plan and budget for it. Just keep pushing ahead. Have fun with it. Work together with some friends, helping them identify their own unique directions and support them in their efforts as they'll support you.

❑ Google your chosen industry.

❑ Set up a Google Alert for legal and business updates using the obvious industry keywords.

❑ Subscribe to some newsletters and blogs.

❑ Read ongoing articles that arrive regularly by email.

❑ Learn the related legal business issues.

❑ Create an industry-focused (a) Twitter handle (e.g. @tirelawyer) and (b) personal profile, and start tweeting occasionally.
   ○ Twitter is a simple, free activity.
   ○ You can dash off the occasional tweet while waiting for class to start.

❑ Create a club.
   ○ Ideally, it would be an "official" law school club, e.g. the "Emory Law School Tire-Law Group."
   ○ If your school won't sanction your club, create one anyway, outside of school, e.g. the "Atlanta Tire-Law Association."
   ○ Invite your friends to join your group or committee.
   ○ Everyone gets an impressive title.
   ○ They also may add it to their own resume.

So, What Should You Do at School?

- ❑ Create a credible online record of your activities.
  - Hold occasional lunch or after-school meetings.
  - Always take photos.
    - Your smartphone's high-resolution camera is sufficient.
  - Create signage or banners to validate the group.
    - If an actual printed banner is too costly, write the group's name neatly on the room's chalkboard or whiteboard.
  - Take turns speaking at the podium with the group name behind you.
  - Post speaking photos all over social media.
    - Don't show the attendees if it's sparse.

- ❑ Hold monthly lunchtime or after-school events.
  - It's easy to find an empty classroom for your meetings.
  - Post the events to social media.

- ❑ Leverage social media.
  - Post the committee notices to Twitter, LinkedIn, and Facebook.
  - Always post the photos to social media.

- ❑ Go on a field trip. For example, find a way to tour a nearby factory or facility connected to the industry.

- ❑ Attend the local professional industry association meetings and conferences.
  - Network. Bring your business cards.
  - Meet the members and leaders. Collect their cards.
    - Enter their information in your contact database or spreadsheet.
  - Within 24 hours, invite the people you meet to connect on LinkedIn.

- ❑ Use Google, Lexis/Nexis, and Westlaw to identify the lawyers who have represented clients in the targeted industry.
  - Seek to connect with them on LinkedIn with an invitation note highlighting your common industry interest.
    - "I see that you have a specialty in representing tire companies. I'm the President of the Emory Tire-Law Club. I'd like to invite you to join my network."

The Ultimate Law Student Get-A-Job Checklist

- That is a much more intriguing and effective invitation to receive than "I'm a law student, can we connect?"
- You're expanding your personal network with movers, shakers, and possible future employers.

☐ Create a simple, free, targeted, blog with WordPress, Wix, Squarespace, etc.
  - Draft occasional blog posts.
    - Once a month is plenty, although more is better.
  - Write short, 250-500-word articles, just one or two double-spaced typed pages.
    - Use simple internet English, written at a 7th-grade level, like *People* magazine.
    - No footnotes or citations.
  - Don't obsess over the details, perfection is paralyzing.
    - No typos
  - Post links to your blogs and your other social media sites.
  - Send links to the lawyers who specialize in this area, and your growing industry network.
  - Cut up the article and post the pieces gradually as individual Tweets too.
    - Remember, you're creating *volume*.

☐ Create an account on slideshare.net
  - Google loves SlideShare.
  - Create a detailed, targeted personal profile.
  - Always include both your general biographical data *and* information detailing your specialty.
    - The specialty area isn't your only interest or ability, consider it an additional area of concentration.

☐ Give a 5-10-minute speech to your Group or Committee.
  - Videotape the presentation in high-definition with your phone.
  - See the "Write, Speak, Repurpose, and Reuse" chapter to create additional materials.

You're not just creating expertise, you're also showing your interest and *passion* for the topic. People want to see your enthusiasm; it's infectious and persuasive.

- ☐ Research the law firms that have these specialties.
  - ○ Use Google and Career Services to identify these firms.
  - ○ Use LinkedIn to identify any connections you have in common.
  - ○ See if they have a local office in your area.

- ☐ Pay attention to the names of the reporters who write about this area in each publication.
  - ○ You'll see that it's typically the same reporters; that's their "beat."
  - ○ Connect with them on LinkedIn and Twitter with personal notes.
  - ○ Reach out to them occasionally with information or tips.

- ☐ Identify members of this focused community.
  - ○ Join any relevant clubs or associations they belong to.
    - • That group might be your best networking opportunity.
  - ○ Seek to give a speech to that group.
  - ○ Post the networking and speaking photos to Twitter, LinkedIn, Facebook, and Instagram.

- ☐ Conduct a search for any unique holidays that you can creatively associate with this effort.
  - ○ For example, if you're interested in admiralty, you can celebrate National Maritime Day or World Maritime Day (both holidays actually exist). I
  - ○ If you're marketing your mining experience, December 6 is National Miners Day.
  - ○ You can find countless obscure, semi-legitimate holidays to celebrate.
    - • Search online for "unique holidays." See, e.g. *www.holidayinsights.com/*

Writing a Persuasive Resume and Cover Letter

Writing a Persuasive Resume and Cover Letter

Your goal is to create a specialty area you enjoy along with some supporting evidence you can use to create the perception of expertise. Then draft a persuasive resume and cover letter that tells that story in a way that gets you more job interviews.

Bulk up your resume with as many simple "hooks" as possible. For example, I went to law school in Atlanta, but wanted a job in Chicago. I realized that having a big-name Chicago law firm on my resume would catch the attention of Chicago hiring professionals. At the time, one of the few Chicago firms with an Atlanta outpost was Lord Bissell & Brook (now Locke Lord). I needed to land a job at Lord Bissell—almost *any* job would do. So, I used my connection to Chicago to get hired as a low-end messenger clerk in their Atlanta office.

But that was okay, I just needed to work up from the bottom of the barrel to the lower-middle of the barrel, to persuade them to let me do almost any sort of legal work that would credibly allow me to say that I "clerked" there. I worked some afternoons, got to know a few lawyers just barely well enough to ask them to let me proofread some of their filings, to gain some actual legal experience. It wasn't high-level experience, but it *was* sufficient to ethically add it to my resume.

Reformat your resume to highlight your unique strengths. Do not feel you must follow the "standard" or "recommended" resume layout.

We're not going to spend a lot of time on resume writing, there is an entire industry dedicated to that topic. The best-known book in this area is "What Color Is Your Parachute? 2019: A Practical Manual for Job-Hunters and Career-Changers." Find it at *http://tinyw.in/BJzf*. Your school's Career Services professionals likely have additional resources available to students. Inquire about them.

In terms of structure and layout of your resume, simply remember that we're trying to grab the attention of someone who's skimming through a thick stack of look-alike resumes. Imagine that your resume is in the middle of a pile of 100 resumes, and you need to capture their attention in a positive way.

They will glance at your materials for a couple seconds and make a snap decision which pile to put you into: Yes, Maybe, or Reject. You need your cover letter and resume to immediately highlight your most-persuasive facts, to fight your way into one of the first two piles.

Use design techniques like location on the page, font size and selection, bold and italics, to direct the reader's attention to your most powerful information and away from your weaknesses. Look at a lot of sample resumes to find the layout that highlights your information best. You can be creative, but don't overdo it.

Smaller firms and organizations will have someone physically sorting through the resume. Larger firms will use technology to automate the first-cut process. The creative techniques I'm advocating will not be as effective with software that can be programmed to sort resumes by class rank or GPA.

If you want a job at those firms, you must aim your networking and communications specifically at the individual lawyers who can bypass their automated system.

That is, you'll need to bypass the firm's Recruiting Manager and directly contact the partner whose practice aligns with the specialty you've built.

Be aware of the word-matching technology that automated systems use to pull relevant resumes from the online forms and stacks of scanned pdfs. If you want a particular type of job, you will want your resume to use the precise words the computer's algorithm has been programmed to search for. Be thoughtful and strategic in the language you use in your resume descriptions, including synonyms.

Many of your targeted readers, the partners at prominent firms perhaps, will not be expecting to receive your resume, so your cover letter must get to the point quickly and clearly. You need to make your case and tell your story right up front. Something like this, perhaps:

Dear Ms. Smith:

My research shows that you have one of the region's leading Tire Law practices. I thought you might find my experience as the founder and president of the Emory Law School Tire-Law Association interesting. I am a third-year law student seeking a job...

Second-Year Students (2Ls)

MINDSET:

Build your external brand and develop your network.

Second-Year Students (2Ls)

By the second year you should have a handle on the law school experience. Do your best to earn good grades but this is a critical year to also build the credentials that can help get you that vital 2L summer job—the one that will provide the experience you can leverage to get that essential first post-graduation full-time job.

Your grades still matter, just not nearly as much if you can refocus or redirect the hiring professional onto something else they'll find equally persuasive. That involves strategy, research, networking, and follow up.

- Continue your "First-Year Students" activities.

- If you are starting now as a 2L, combine the "First-Year Students" and "Second-Year Students (2L's)" activities.

- Stay in touch with your friends and contacts.

- Continue adding new names to your mailing list and to your LinkedIn networks as you meet new contacts.
  - Your fellow law students
  - Bar association committee members
  - Professionals you meet at networking and industry functions

- Join LinkedIn groups of the associations and industries you are involved or interested in.
  - Pay attention to the conversations.
  - Learn the industry leaders.

- Read legal-profession trade magazines and law-specific blogs and news sources to develop greater substantive skills. Some of our favorites are:
  - abovethelaw.com
  - ms-jd.org
  - The American Bar Association, Law Student Committee

- Create Your Own Journal. Some of my Emory law school friends had a good idea—if their grades weren't going to get them on Law Review, they'd start their own.

- They liked bankruptcy law and saw a gap in the marketplace. So, they talked to the school and got approval to launch the *Emory Bankruptcy Developments Journal.* http://law.emory.edu/ebdj/index.html
    - And as Editors of what looked like a prestigious law journal, they all got good jobs in New York and Atlanta.
    - Remarkably, 30 years later, the *EBDJ* is still running!
- A formally sanctioned law school journal is impressive—and a lot of work. Not as noteworthy but much easier would be creating a blog with a "Journal" or "Review" title.

Third-Year Students (3Ls)

MINDSET:

Continue developing your external network within your specialty area.

Add more elements to your resume.

Interact directly with individual lawyers and professionals at the organizations where you'd like to work after graduation.

Third-Year Students (3Ls)

- ☐ Continue the First- and Second-Year Students activities, above.

- ☐ If you're just starting to think and strategize about getting a job now, it's not too late, but I'd recommend that you get *aggressive* in building your experience and resume.
    - Review the activities identified in the previous chapters and start adding as many as you can, as quickly as possible.
    - Building an impressive resume takes time, so start by adding the easiest and most-persuasive activities first.

- ☐ Engage frequently with your Career Services office.
    - They are most likely connected to the school's alumni and can provide introductions to those who might be in a position to assist.

- ☐ Continue building practical legal experience with a part-time legal job or clinic.

- ☐ Third-year classes are generally easier; your load is lighter. Your primary job now is to find a full-time job.
    - Devote more time to building your resume and networking.

- ☐ Participate more actively in your chosen industry association.
    - Volunteer for a committee and work toward a leadership position.
    - Write a brief article on an area of interest for a committee newsletter.
    - Give another short speech on an area of particular interest.
        - Trim, edit, and reuse the video and content as described in the "Write, Speak, Repurpose, and Reuse" section above.

- ☐ Increase your marketing efforts; devote some time each week to a proactive networking activity, e.g., lunch, breakfast, dinner, sports, professional events, etc.

- ☐ Master a basic "elevator speech."
    - There are many good sources of how-to information available online.
    - Learn to position your description in a memorable, personal way.

The Ultimate Law Student Get-A-Job Checklist

- ○ Write multiple versions of your elevator pitch to use depending upon the context and audience. That is, only use your Tire Law focus with those who care about that industry.
- ○ Develop separate summaries that detail both your (1) general experience and (2) specialty area.
  - Quick version: One or two sentences
  - Medium version: One to two paragraphs; an expansion of your quick version
  - Long version: An expansion of your medium version; can include example experiences and other relevant information
  - Alternative versions: Create customized versions of your elevator pitch for different audiences

☐ Attend marketing and business-development training offered by your school.
- ○ If your school doesn't offer it, request it.
- ○ Many prominent law schools are offering marketing and business-development training to their students.
- ○ See the video at *https://goo.gl/4RxHNp*

☐ Read legal and targeted industry publications, print and online. Stay current on the issues relevant to your chosen field.
- ○ Subscribe to blogs and follow Twitter accounts of leaders in these areas.

☐ Create Google Alerts of people and companies in your field (e.g., "Fishman Marketing").
- ○ Use information you receive as a reason to contact or congratulate.

☐ Continue regularly updating your LinkedIn profile.
- ○ Add new organizations, volunteering experience, and honors and awards.
- ○ Add your top thought-leadership pieces to the Publications section and include a summary and the article URL.

☐ Expand your network and build your external reputation and resume.
- ○ Focus on building relationships with lawyers who target

that industry and industry professionals who could become clients later in your career.

- ❏ Learn about the leading companies in your chosen industry.
  - ○ Regularly read industry websites, publications, and blogs.
  - ○ Conduct online research periodically to stay current on their issues and needs.
  - ○ Browse company websites regularly, especially sections like "About Us," "What's New," and "Press Releases."
  - ○ Follow them on LinkedIn and Twitter.

- ❏ Write an article for a legal or industry publication or blog on new issues, trends, or precedents relevant to your chosen specialty.
  - ○ You may also use the article as an opportunity to get a meeting with a valuable lawyer or hiring partner.
    - "I'm writing an article on [XYZ] and I need to quote an expert on this topic. Could I stop by your office to interview you for the article next week?"
    - It's a nice personal touch that will enable you to stay in contact and give you a connection and advantage on hiring opportunities.

- ❏ Continue adding to your LinkedIn network with friends and professional contacts.

- ❏ Work toward a leadership position in your selected industry association.
  - ○ Use technology to help grow and stay in touch with your network, e.g., blogs, Twitter, LinkedIn, etc.

- ❏ On LinkedIn, endorse the professionals you meet.

- ❏ Request LinkedIn Recommendations as appropriate.
  - ○ Write sincere Recommendations for your best connections and prospects.

- ❏ If you enjoy Twitter, follow the journalists who cover your chosen specialty area.
  - ○ Engage with them occasionally.

- Build relationships with journalists who may ask you to act as a resource for articles.
  - Others who follow those journalists may follow you too.

On a final note, if your goal is to practice law after law school, passing the bar exam is a vital step to consider during your 3L year.

❏ Take advantage of any bar-review programs your school offers.

❏ Consider your school's historic bar-passage rate.
  - If your school has a relatively low passage rate (or you will be taking the bar in a state with a notoriously difficult bar exam) and you haven't secured employment by the time bar-prep starts, consider putting your search on hold and dedicate all your time and attention to passing the bar exam.

❏ Failing to pass the bar exam will set your career back, so it's important to do your best to pass on your first try.
  - If you don't pass, use the time until your next attempt to continue enhancing the resume that will help get you that great job.
  - At this point, it is a good idea to seek out advice from a bar exam expert to ensure that the next time you take the exam you will pass.

If you follow this checklist, over time you will create a resume that shows you as an exceptional, energetic, hard-working, and dedicated student, one with unique skills they can't find in the piles of look-alike resumes clogging their desks and in-boxes. You'll stand out in a positive way.

You'll also find that this same niche and network you developed will be an enormous benefit to you some years down the road, because you will be more likely to be able to turn those contacts into clients. You will already know them well. They'll trust you. You won't be one more gluttonous lawyer snuggling up to them to get their legal business.

Rather, you'll be a helpful friend, a valued member of their professional community whom they've known for many years. You'll be the lawyer who hasn't been persistently begging for their business, which will make it more likely that you'll be able to get it later. You already invested time in the relationships, you'll find success with them well into your years in practice.

And, you will have laid the foundation for a successful career, one that is fulfilling personally, professionally, and financially.

Remember, once you identify what you love to do, find a way to bring that into your practice. If you do, you may spend the decades until retirement leaping out of bed every morning absolutely passionate about your profession, your career, and your success.

Of course, your first law job may not be your ideal job, but that's OK. Get the best job you can and see where it leads. It's just the first step on a long, winding path that will last any number of decades. Try to last at least 2-3 years at that first job before jumping ship.

Work hard. Do your best. Learn everything you can from it. You may find that it becomes a stepping stone toward the next job that leads to an even brighter future. You're building the skills and the personal network that will eventually help you land where you want to be.

General Mindset

General Mindset

Once you land that job, never do the minimum. Always do more than is expected. Get to work a bit earlier, stay a little later. Pay attention to how the partners are dressed. Ensure that your shoes are shined and your clothing is neat and clean. Show that you care, that you take this important profession seriously and are dedicated to doing your best for the firm and its clients.

Clients can't always tell whether you're doing a good technical job, but they can tell how well you're treating them. Communicate regularly. Meet your obligations and deadlines. Be responsive—don't make clients wait to hear from you; try to return every call within two hours and never let a call or email go unreturned overnight.

Treat every person at the firm with the utmost respect regardless of whether they're a lawyer or support staff. Learn the names of all of the receptionists, secretaries, clerks, and messengers. It's not only the decent thing to do, people notice. It matters.

It is very important to take care of yourself. Law can be a difficult and stressful career. We work long hours on intellectually and emotionally challenging projects for clients who may seem demanding and unappreciative. Depression and substance abuse are statistically significant issues among law students and young lawyers.

If you feel that you may need some support or assistance, there are many available resources designed specifically for lawyers. These include (1) Lawyer Assistance Programs through state and local bar associations and (2) the renowned Hazelden Betty Ford Foundation at *www.hazeldenbettyford.org/*. Seek them out.

Eat right and get enough sleep and exercise. Ensure you have a vibrant life outside of law school and your legal practice as well. Spend time with your friends and family, and don't neglect your hobbies and outside interests. Volunteer for a charity. Consider reading *The Happiness Advantage* by Shawn Anchor, which discusses how "happiness fuels success." In your life and career, strive for a career that provides *both*.

I wish you all the best of luck, happiness, and success in your chosen profession.

The End.

"And will you succeed?
Yes! You will, indeed!
(98 and ¾ percent guaranteed.)
   KID, YOU'LL MOVE MOUNTAINS!"

Oh, the Places You'll Go!
Dr. Seuss

Addendum

DRAFTING A PERSUASIVE LINKEDIN PROFILE

1. List Your Full Name

Do not use abbreviations. Married women who changed their name should include their maiden name as well.

2. Display a Professional Photo

There are reasons why some people don't want to display their photos, but this is a social networking platform. Not displaying your photo raises more questions than provides answers. Ensure that it is a professional, high-quality photograph. LinkedIn is not Facebook; do not use cropped group, vacation, or wedding photos. No props or artistic effects. Express your personality but err on the side being more conservative. Below are three LinkedIn photos with different styles. Iris Jones is outside with natural lighting and casual but professional attire. Rob Fishman is in a business-casual shirt in a work setting that feels friendly and informal. Samantha Ruben wears a business suit with a traditional solid-colored background that looks like a formal photo shoot. Each photograph conveys slightly different impressions. Choose your photo to support the image you are trying to create.

3. Have a Headline That Properly Brands You

In the space underneath your name is your "Professional" or Profile Headline. It will appear in search results next to your name, as well as next to any questions you ask or answer. It is, in essence, your elevator pitch in a few words. Do not simply put your title and firm name here: this is the place to interest anyone who finds you in a LinkedIn search result to learn more about you. Think more in terms of "UNC Law Student interested in Tax Law" rather than "Law Student".

4. Have Something Relevant and Timely in Your Status Update

The Status Update is about showing that you are still relevant in doing whatever you are doing. Going to an event? Share it. Attending a conference? Share it. Read something interesting that is relevant to your brand? Share it. Use your Status Update to show your relevance and try to aim for a once-a-week update. You don't want someone visiting your profile and see a status update that is months old. For those who enjoy writing, LinkedIn is an ideal platform to push out your articles.

5. Display Enough Work Experience... with Details

Your LinkedIn profile doesn't need to be a resume. One simple sentence summarizing what you did is enough to ensure that a potential reader understands the role that you had. Job descriptions provide you the perfect opportunity to pepper your profile with narrow, search engine-friendly keywords that will help you get found. For example:

> Amber concentrates her practice in the area of litigation, with a primary emphasis on litigating large commercial disputes. She regularly represents financial institutions, corporations, limited liability companies, and individuals in contract, corporate, shareholder, U.C.C., and fiduciary disputes in all of the federal and state courts of North Carolina, including the North Carolina Business Court.

6. Education

Put education details on your profile. What did you achieve at a certain school? Honors, awards, or activities? Mention them.

7. Get Some Recommendations

The LinkedIn "profile completeness" algorithm requires that you receive three recommendations in order to get to 100%. This is not critical but is useful. Do not be embarrassed to ask friends who know you well to recommend you; it's a well-understood part of social networking today. If you've done a particularly good job at an internship don't be afraid to ask a supervisor or colleague for a recommendation. Email them the link, to make it easier for them. And of course, it's only polite to recommend them back!

8. Acquire Connections

If you're on LinkedIn you should be networking. Connections are also important to help get found in the huge LinkedIn database. Rule of thumb? Multiply your age by 10 and that is the *minimum* number of connections that you should have. Join some relevant practice and industry groups and connect with the members you know. Start with your law school class and firms you've interned at. Connect, connect, connect.

9. Your Professional Summary is *Essential*

The Professional Summary section is the first thing people will read, right after your headline. Don't just dump the first 2,000 characters of your standard resume into your LinkedIn Summary. This is how you will introduce yourself to your professional contacts and future employers. This is the most-important professional social-networking platform, so why not spend a few minutes introducing yourself? This is the place for you to tell your own story, in your own voice, typically with a bit more personality than you can show on a resume.

Devote the time necessary to make your Summary truly great. Admittedly it can be difficult to write this way about yourself, so get some help if necessary from a professional writer, or perhaps an old friend who aced that college creative writing class.

Here's one I wrote for my friend Joe Fasi, one of the nation's top trial lawyers. Joe's a terrific, modest guy, and he wins complex ten-figure cases because juries like and trust him. It's just 333 words long, but see if after reading this you are starting to like and trust him a bit already:

> Most people know the movie "The Maltese Falcon." I am not the Maltese Falcon, but I am from the island of Malta and speak fluent Maltese. I also like to speak to jurors, and do so often and in cases with large damages at stake. I've tried over 100 jury trials to verdict, defending complex cases with enormous exposure against sympathetic plaintiffs.
>
> I haven't counted up my precise win-loss record, but a client recently asked me "how the heck I keep winning all these cases." I wasn't exactly sure how to respond to that, but I smiled and thanked him for what he intended as a compliment. Thinking about it later, I suspect the answer might partly be that I don't get involved in the games that many litigators like to play. I don't play puerile hide-the-ball tricks. I'm aggressive, but honest and reasonable. I want a fair and just resolution and, if a plaintiff wants my client to pay a lot of money, they better prove that they're darn well entitled to every penny of it.
>
> In post-trial research, juries have universally said that they liked me — they felt I approached the trial with decency and integrity, and trusted me to help them get at the truth. This is particularly important because it means I become the face of the faceless corporation. I've helped level the playing field.
>
> Fewer and fewer large cases actually go to trial. When they do, I defend them, nationwide, for companies that are among the most skilled and strategic purchasers of legal services, including manufacturers, pharmaceutical, and tobacco.

I typically handle cases as the lead trial attorney, getting hired at the outset to resolve a problematic dispute or lawsuit. Some companies use me as a their "go-to attorney," parachuting me in on the courthouse steps, either to support an existing trial team, or simply take over and handle the trial, especially the large or challenging cases.

Specialties: Product Liability, defense of nursing homes, and professional/medical liability.

11. Claiming Your Personal URL

When you sign up to LinkedIn you are provided a complex "Public URL." You can customize and simplify this when you edit your profile with a couple simple steps. If you have a common name, make sure you claim your URL before others do! My LinkedIn URL is *linkedin.com/in/rossfishman/*.

It's simple, and yours should be too. You can then include your abbreviated LinkedIn link on your email signature, business card, and everywhere else you go online. A quick Google search will find short videos detailing the simple steps.

12. Website

You can add up to three website links. You will want to link to your blog or other social media networks that you are using professionally.

13. Join Groups

You should join Groups that are relevant to your areas of interest and expertise, get active in the discussions to help meet people in your growing professional network, build your brand as a helpful and knowledgeable member of the community, and start connecting with the members as mentioned above.

HOW TO WRITE FOR THE INTERNET AND ENHANCE YOUR SEO

Biographies, LinkedIn pages, blog posts, and other online material can and should be used to elevate your rankings on search engines like Google (called Search-Engine Optimization, or SEO).

We know roughly what Google's algorithms are looking for, which makes it possible to draft your materials in a way that uses this information to improve your results. Although there are no guarantees and the rules continue to change, leveraging this information and staying current on the trends and updates improves your chance of being found by your target audience of potential employers.

Fundamentally, Google tries to connect each search with the specific pages on credible websites that seem to best match that search. Therefore, when drafting the pages you would like ranked highly by Google, write from the perspective of a prospect seeking that information, working backwards from the specific Google searches they would conduct. Consider the exact terms they would use in the search box and use that same language in your online materials, like websites, LinkedIn, and other social media.

These days, sophisticated users are conducting longer, more complex searches, including narrow specialty areas or identifying particular types of contracts, clauses, phrases, or statutes. They include the name of the city, county, or state, which means you should also if you want to persuade Google that your page is highly relevant.

Here is one of the most-important pieces of information in this area:

There are no "actual" Google search results—results differ on every computer. Google basically knows who and where you are and tries to tailor the results to be most helpful to what you're probably looking for. This means that your search results will be very different from someone conducting the exact same search down the hall or in a different city or country. It's why when you search for "Plumber" you'll see plumbers in your local geographic area and not from Paris or Sao Paulo.

This reality can lead to biased results and a false confidence in your success. When you conduct a general "organic" search, your website may receive a high ranking because Google knows your personal search history and your previous interest in that website. But a more objective or disinterested searcher, like a prospect searching from a different city, might not find you on Google at all.

Author Biographies

Ross Fishman, J.D.

"Of Counsel" magazine wrote: "Many people consider Ross to be the nation's foremost expert on law firm marketing."

Ross is one of the legal profession's most-popular marketing, business-development, and CLE keynote speakers and trainers, having presented 300 times to law firms, law schools, bar associations, and other organizations in 25 countries. Ross's entertaining and educational presentations draw on his experience as a lawyer, marketing director, and marketing partner, inspiring professionals at all levels. See his speaker website at *rossfishman.com*.

A Fellow of the College of Law Practice Management and a Kentucky Colonel, Ross has received innumerable international marketing awards for his law firm branding and websites initiatives for leading law firms and associations worldwide.

He has written 300 bylined articles and six popular marketing books and was the very first marketer inducted into the international Legal Marketing Association's Hall of Fame. Subscribe to his marketing blog at *fishmanmarketing.com/blog*.

A 1986 member of the federal Trial Bar (N.D. Ill.), Ross received a B.A. in Speech Communications from the University of Illinois, and his J.D. from Emory University School of Law.

ross@fishmanmarketing.com
fishmanmarketing.com
LinkedIn.com/in/rossfishman
Twitter: *@rossfishman*

Kerriann Stout, Esq.

Kerriann Stout is the founder and CEO of Vinco, a bar exam-coaching company that helps law students pass the bar exam with less stress and more confidence. In her 5+ years in legal education, Kerriann has helped hundreds of students successfully navigate the difficulties of surviving law school and the bar exam. Kerriann regularly writes and presents on all things related to law school and the bar exam. You can follow her weekly column at "Above the Law" at *https://abovethelaw.com/author/kerriannstout*.

A proud native New York, Kerriann earned her B.A. in Modern Languages, *magna cum laude*, from Pace University, and her J.D., *cum laude*, from The Elisabeth Haub School of Law at Pace University. She continues to live, work, and play in New York.

info@vincoprep.com
www.vincoprep.com
Linkedin.com/in/kerriannstout

Acknowledgments

Acknowledgments

The Ultimate Law Students Get-a-Job Checklist was 30+ years in the making. It was initially based upon my law school experience and memories working as a fresh-faced litigator at a mid-sized law firm that offered marketing training to associates. Then I layered 25 years of law marketing and branding experience on top.

I am deeply grateful to my subject-matter editor, Kerriann Stout, who provided diligent insight into the current state of the law students' market and mindset. I also appreciate the many suggestions I've received from lawyers, law students, marketers, and Career Services professionals, many of which I adapted to enhance the quality of the material. And a special thanks to our assiduous copy editor, Andrew Fishman.

And during each new update and iteration, I sought input from industry experts who selflessly volunteered their unique perspectives. I am especially grateful to the professionals listed below whose personal insight helped inform this current version. My sincere thanks go out to them:

Hollis R Hanover, J.D.
Associate Director of Career Services
Loyola University Chicago School of Law

Shawn P. McKenna, J.D.
Director of Employer Outreach
University of North Carolina School of Law

Robin Thorner, J.D.
Director of the Office of Career Services
St. Mary's University School of Law

Melanie Helene Andersen, LL.M
Law graduate, University of Southern Denmark, 2018
Odense, Denmark

www.ingramcontent.com/pod-product-compliance
Lightning Source LLC
Chambersburg PA
CBHW071207220526
45468CB00002B/538